YOU

YOU

VANE LASHUA

ARPress
ILLUMINATING IDEAS
EMPOWERING VOICES

ARPress
45 Dan Road Suite 5
Canton MA 02021
Hotline: 1(888) 821-0229
Fax: 1(508) 545-7580

Ordering Information:
Quantity sales. Special discounts are available on quantity purchases by corporations, associations, and others. For details, contact the publisher at the address above.

Printed in the United States of America.

ISBN-13:	Softcover	979-8-89330-838-9
	eBook	979-8-89330-839-6

Library of Congress Control Number: 2024902582

"Vane Lashua has a very diverse and rich background in a variety of technical and administrative positions encompassing a long and successful career. He also has a very keen interest in and dedication to the sustainability of our planet and a deep knowledge of the technical issues around clean energy. In addition, he is a very warm and gentle mannered person."

Jane Kolleeny, Garrison Institute. Garrison, NY.

"For six years, I have worked with Vane Lashua in two roles. First in his highly respected role as a Commissioner on the New York State Bridge Authority's governing board, Mr. Lashua was always keenly knowledgeable and actively engaged in his many important responsibilities overseeing the complex finances and inner workings of an infrastructure organization.

Second, as a founding member of Historic Bridges of the Hudson Valley (HBHV), he shepherded a new non-profit organization to a pivotal and important role in regional schools and libraries. As an educator he was able to guide and support the development of this organization to produce highly interactive teacher tools including a "Traveling Museum" and a "Virtual Museum. [Vane]'s energy, enthusiasm and expertise [has been] a great asset."

Tara Sullivan, NY State Bridge Authority

Table of Contents

YOU 1

AND WACKY AM I..3

ALL THE BIRDS ARE GONE 4

THE SEED...5

CIRCUMSTANCE AND SYNCRONICITY 6

MY DEEPEST FEAR 6

BREAKING AWAY – THE LITTLE 500 7

CO-INCIDENCE 10

SOMEONE ELSE'S PATH 10

QUELQUEFOIS..10

1966..11

MY COUNTRY, 'TIS OF THEE...12

STATIC COMES WITH THE RADIO....................................12

I TOOK A WALK TODAY 13

FROM ART WE CANNOT WANDER 13

IN A CEMETERY COMES..14

CONVERSATIONS WITH DONALD HALL AND BOB DYLAN 14

BASTILLE DAY 15

LOCK IT UP!..17

POOR ME (ALWAYS WORKING) 18

DOWNTOWN 18

RORRIM..19

CARS, TRUCKS AND REBEL FLAGS 19

FEEDING INSTRUCTIONS..20

TALKING TO MYSELF 22

THE SHADOW OF THE OBJECT FALLING ON THE EGO 22

THE BUS 23

GRAVITY...24

ALEXANDER TECHNIQUE...25

GOLF..25

WORLD NEWS TONIGHT (2002) 31

AM I DAVID? 33

WHERE AM I? 34

BIG BANG...35

RIVER OF LOVE 36

SEVENTH WAVE...36

I TOOK A WALK TODAY 37

BOOKTALK 38

DANCER 40

AFTERMATH A MEMORY -- THE LOVERS 41

IN THE WOODS 42

GRAVITY..43

VACUUM 44

JOBHUNT..45

A NIGHT YOU NEEDED ME..47

HOW'S JACK? 48

CHIMERA 49

CONNIE'SBIRTHADDRESS 50

FICTION 51

MOCKINGBIRD 51

GIRL WITH A PEARL EARRING......................................52

PARABOLIC CURVES 52

SUBURBAN THERAPY 53

A VISION 57

I DON'T KNOW...57

VACKRA SVENSKA FLICKOR 58

SUE 59

GINNA 59

JUNE..59

TESS...60

EGG NOG..61

INGREDIENTS...64

YOU
By W.H. Auden

Really, must you,
Overfamiliar
Dense companion,
Be there always?
The bond between us
Is chimerical, surely,
Yet I cannot break it.
Must I, born for sacred play,
Turn base mechanic
So you may worship
Your secular bread
With no sense
Of the value of time?
Thus far I have seen your
Character only
From its pleasanter side,
But you know I know,
A day will come
When you go savage
And hurt me badly.
Totally stupid?
Would you were!
But, no, you plague me
With tastes I was fool enough
Once to believe in:
Bah, blockhead,
I know where you learned them.
Can I trust you even
On creaturely facts?
I suspect strongly
You hold some dogma
Of Positive Truth
And feed me fictions:
I shall never prove it.
Oh, I know how you came by

A sinner's cranium,
How between two glaciers
The master-chronometer
Of an innocent primate
Altered its tempi:
That explains nothing.
Who tinkered and why?
Why am I certain,
Whatever your faults are,
The faults are mine?
Why is loneliness not
A chemical discomfort
Nor being a smell?

AND WACKY AM I

And now wacky am I, I thank you, mother, for
the days I take no pill;

the oak table that folds upon itself,
a hinge, a turn, a hidden box
containing nothing, a silence left to me alone;

the vaporous song echoing here from the
dusty floor of a small house
in a village like so many.

I thank you that I somehow sing
though rhythms and their verses
keep note and meaning but to me,

through the doubt that song to my self
in silence be song at all.

March, 2009

ALL THE BIRDS ARE GONE

Robins' nest is empty, all dreamin' done today.
All the birds are gone, and the sky is gray;

Fledgling Wilbur flew the nest, then Oliver flapped away.
The yard below the nest was fenced, so mom could train & play,
no dogs to chase the fledges and make'em playin' prey.
But giving worms to encourage the two who remained to stay,
accidentally moved them to claw out, dive and go on their way.
One ran toward the road, so with imitation wings & ludicrous human
    display,
I herded her back toward shelter in the dog & human fray.
At first panicked, robin mom & partners dove & threatened with their
    warning bray.
But seeing my intentions, mom's wondrous posse "joined",
and pressed the young'n' to shelter beneath a leafy spray.

All the birds are gone now, and the sky is gray.
The family she mothered, her selfless display, her partners gone,
but the love and joy she rendered, are alive and all regrets allay.

THE SEED

I watch in 3D, yes, even without TV,
a flutter so ordinary, so extr'ordinary
because I have to watch, then dream, imagine,
travel new paths, beyond my sedentation, beyond my education;
Every minute, every day, I remain in wonder.
Around me lies miracle, yet all is ordinaire;
even this seed, even this tree, even the life its seed hath wrought
    floating down in air to reality.
Every vein, every root in memory, planted by the seed to seek
the ordinary mystery in the never- and unknown,
to wet its being, to feed the self as it grows to be, whose shared
    community brings forth
the corpulent beginning of a vein turned to a being, toward neighbors
and simple place,
to feed itself, its leaves, its bark, its invitation to share and seek its
    neighbors --
all from the beings who compose its legacy and ours
all in magical verse within its seed.
Though we cannot read its, as it cannot read ours, we share the wonder
    and inevitable nature of life in community,
all wrought seed by seed,
reading together, growing stronger as one ...
and yet, only having grown through the gifts of each other
and our shared earthen species together from a single seed
and the mystery that has lain before and lies beyond.

CIRCUMSTANCE AND SYNCRONICITY

Each moment of one's life is preparation;
both this moment and infinite moments to come,
gathered become momentous, moments' preparation,
behind the glass are lost; before, become aspiration,
perspiration realized, sweat.

MY DEEPEST FEAR

is that I only know what I can look up.
My greatest pride is remembering what I have learned.
I find more tattered fragments than I find whole cloth, lately,
    and find familiar tears in warp and weave.
My greatest fear is that I waste my cosmic purpose,
re-using rehearsed threads come again
of pattern imagined or real, unwittingly echoed.
I am keen to make some colossal record at-bats of no-repeat thoughts,
    but fear and fear and fear.
Great recurring themes all easy to come by are regrets, power, energy,
    family, my child, children, food, the sun, mechanics, life's insistent
    wonder, unexpected visual pleasure, the connection of visual recall
    to physical reaction, my father, the farm, natural edges, colors of the
    praying mantis, flight, chaos, a word I learned for describing the artful
    ease with which we recognize our awful differences with men and our
    sensuous and alluring ones with women, (competition straight and
    simple), pride, context, words, movement, hunger, disease, simple
    harmony, disjuncture and sloth.

BREAKING AWAY – THE LITTLE 500

Before Dave Blaze, who was the inspiration for Steve Tesich's *Breaking Away*, Little 500 riders were mostly athletes using their physical talent on a bike, rather than cyclists. Training for the Little 500 meant losing a season of something else or jumping up a notch into serious training. The Little 500 race itself was just the last 50 miles of a long, tough, and wonderful personal experience that in the '60s lasted from December till the race in May.

Riding in the Little 500 creates a bond not only between the members of the team and those who support it (coaches, mechanics, timers and such), but with all those who ride the course. This bonding happens in most sports or other rites of passage – like living in the Beta house.

Meanwhile, a particular memory returns me to Bloomington and reminds me of the incredible joy of being a part of the Little 500, Indiana, and Beta Theta Pi every time it occurs.

To train for the race, our regimen included quarter-mile sprints, track time, relays and exchange work, and lots of time on the road. We worked out in the old fieldhouse over the winter, were just getting into passable form in early March, and just starting to ride together on the road. We sometimes rode alone because of schedules or before our "official" practice began.

One day riding the road to Lake Lemon alone, I saw four riders up ahead dressed in identical light blue sweats. It was the Figi team. They were known contenders and I drove myself to catch up to them so I could catch a breath in the draft behind their line, and I probably had some idea about showing them that we Betas were the team to beat – again in '65.

While I was catching up to them, I noticed they were doing a "loop draft" where the first rider in a line drops back to last, the riders move up, and each rider leads regularly every fourth change. They were riding in as tight a group as possible. I gradually realized that they were changing positions on the clock, maybe every 60 seconds on a signal from one of the riders with a stopwatch. It was a neat discipline and pretty to watch. From a distance their position switching made the group look like a single machine.

The bikes we rode then were heavy, single geared AMF RoadMasters. What they lacked in innovative technology, they made up for in overengineering. The brakes were in the rear hub and operated by backpedaling slightly. The chunking noise of braking in a large group was a constant chatter. The wheels, frame, gear sprockets and chains were heavy and noisy instruments. The seething hum of chains on gears was like background music on every ride. It was small consolation for not having a nice, light 10-speed.

The leading rider in a pack is always pulling harder, breaking the way through the wind. Trailing riders tuck in behind the leader to save energy. If the wind is coming from any point ahead, the lead rider may be working 20 or 30 percent harder than the trailers.

It was an unspoken rule of good form that trailing riders in a pack continue to pedal in synch with the leader without resting or braking. Braking meant wasting energy. Unexpected braking is dangerous to the riders behind who are tucked in close. It is actually easier to continue to rotate the pedals going up a gentle grade, but somewhat harder physical work; while going down a grade, pedaling for speed and staying in synch without handbrakes requires intense concentration. It's a trip.

I pulled up behind the line of bikes and stayed in back of them in fifth position, synching up for a couple of their changes. They were pushing themselves to "hup up" as a team trying to gain energy on every change. As we rode along, I think they almost forgot I was back there. I recognized for a bunch of reasons that I couldn't join their perfectly working machine. But I also felt that staying in the fifth spot or peeling off and going the other way was going to lead to humiliation and/or guilt. So I wound myself up, jumped out of line and sprinted.

As I passed the line of riders, I must have surprised them or woke them up and they got juiced, too. I was fresher than the lead rider because of having drafted a while, but as I jumped out to pass, the leader noticed my move. Though I got slightly ahead, he had picked up the pace. That made it so I couldn't quite draw in, in front, so I stayed on the lead, but beside the lead rider. Just then, the riding timer called time for their lead change. As a courtesy, I churned harder and pushed wider to let the leader swing out and fall back. Then I sprinted a bit, and got out front about 25 yards by myself. It's a subtle delight to show your tail to a pack of hard working riders.

For the next few minutes I managed to stay ahead of the line and they stayed on their timed changes, but they were soon pulling up, right on my wheel. I didn't have a prayer of staying in front very long. I didn't want to collapse, either, though I was doing a respectable enough job that I wouldn't lose face if I fell back and rested in their draft again. But as it happened, the mental dynamic changed as I had taken the lead. None of the riders wanted to remain a part of that machine.

About that time we also must have hit a generally downhill stretch of road, because the next 10 or 15 minutes became effortless. The Figi line just broke up and we all started racing in a swarm, probably faster than I had ever run a bike on flat ground. The shape and texture of a pod of riders changes with the turns in the road, the grade, the wind, but I'm sure nobody was aware of it. There was definitely no traffic on the road, or we would have all been killed. During those few minutes, the only thing I experienced was pure joy.

That was a life lesson and what the experience was all about. I realized that we were helping each other, that we couldn't race without each other; that the better the other guy is, the better I am. We were all of one mind, innocent of everything else, just going through the air as fast as we could go. The way it's supposed to be. No matter what you're doing.

When we finally started to pay attention to the world again, with traffic and muddy shoulders to lookout for on the long downstretch north of IU Stadium, the sun was sun going down, glaring off the road in one of Bloomington's graying, early spring sunsets. There was nothing to do but laugh.

All in all, that's what hooked me on riding in the Little 500. Every racing moment was worth the effort it took to get there. Though I never excelled in competition, my experience in riding was excellent. I wish you all the most excellent of seasons and grades and on and on.

CO-INCIDENCE

Incident by incident flashes by, each bound in expectation as those
    imagined.
Bound in orbits, gamed each one of purposed lives, of loves, of
    incidence and profit,
Bound close by incident memories day by day.
Bound in daily wonder decades long.
Bound, compelled by physics present in our supple times,
binding somehow stronger than the potent gravity of our yearning,
distant, sterile orbits of co-incident desire,
memories, dreams and wondrous shared reality unrealized.

SOMEONE ELSE'S PATH

Here I walk on someone else's path;
I follow the curves, I follow the rules,
I stay in the lines.
Though I venture to improve the path a bit;
Trying to take and perhaps remake its most efficient way,
Still I walk someone else's path.

QUELQUEFOIS

Quelquefois les forces de nature
viennent dans la nuit
et quand ils me relevent,
un indigene
flesh and bones, guts and all,
I am brought to my senses
in the quiet tribal air in forest, light, mist, stream, and
fecund earth unparceled
from my body.
Et quelquefois les forces me réveillent —
ce corps, cet homme, ce nuit, ces bruits.

1966

In 1965 I rode in the Indiana University Little 500 with my Beta Theta Pi fraternity brothers, Phil Goddard, Steve Taylor, and Brock Blosser ('65). Our coaches were Dick Anglin and Jerry Rosner. Brock had become engaged to Karen Checkley ('67) in 1964. Because he was in ROTC, after graduation in 1965, he was made Lieutenant, active duty, assigned to serve in Munich, Germany. Meanwhile, during the next year, I rode on the 1966 Beta team. A number of our brothers decided that in the summer after the 1966 race, we would escort Karen to Munich to be married to Brock – so we made arrangements and made it happen.

After the wedding Brock & Karen left on his 23 day military leave for their honeymoon. The escort team decided to tour Europe separately and meet up in Paris for our flight home in late July. David Evans ('68) and I bought a used VW bug and began a remarkable tour of Europe, first to Vienna then Italy, Monaco, Nice (long story), the Cote d'Azur, Barcelona, Mallorca, back through Andorra, the Pyrenees, to Chartres and on to Paris. Our final stop was a youth hostel located in an elementary school near the Paris Odeon metro stop. Two weeks later, as we gathered at the airport to go home, I waved goodbye to the group and decided to take an offer I had received from the rector of the American Church in Nice for residence in the rectory and tuition-paid study at the Centre universitaire méditerranéen (CUM), well-known for French studies.

Each stop had its own story, of course, and am working on a book inclusive. After the year in Nice, I returned to IU and "made up" hours through summer school and 67-68 so that I could graduate onschedule in 1968. David and I re-met at our 50th reunion in 2018!

MY COUNTRY, 'TIS OF THEE

My country, 'tis of thee,
If thou hadst the least of integrity,
of strength and of courageous intensity,
Thy leaders all, all me and we
the people and our varied religiosity --
beliefs, intentions, focus and perversity --
could make peace worldwide without war;
could invite our friends and "enemies", near and far
with respect to sit with us without fear, on par,
asking all to share beliefs, intent, humanity, needs and more.

What do we want? Why must desire be met or "Kill!"?
Why can we not forgo our selfish wants when our abounding riches
    will?
Why do we hide behind our richly funded towers, walls and corporate
    war machine
Selling death, while we imagine we imagine peace, love, a wonderful
    world and nothing so obscene.

STATIC COMES WITH THE RADIO

Ahhhh, riding down the road at night in an open car.
Turn on the brights to see the deer and a big moth carving
long sinusoidals in the headlight road toward Mars.

Oh, the beautiful cicada music wack-wacking amongst the whirring
    tires,
the poles thup thrupping climb-spike jagged rips and tears
beside the blacktop you know will break again the dangling wires

Cars, mars, tires, wires, comes my roady nightly woo
bump tha-dump into the yellow double splutty stew
while on the windshield splatter tsst tsst of myriad, deadly spew.

Static comes with the radio.

I TOOK A WALK TODAY

I took a walk today down by the canal, in sunshine along the rails
I tight-roped the tracks and timed the ties to step along the day.
I took a walk today, by my magnificent river,
up and down the city hills,
I reason an excuse for rolling fields, for locusts, cattle, sycamores and
    parks.
I took a walk today to open up my spirit, to give me time.
Time to fly, time to recognize my ignorance,
Time to open myself up to all my possibilities,
Time to stop thinking of them and every detail in between.
I love where I am because it is where I am.
I love to watch, to look, to have this Earth around me.
I love to walk in sunshine, rain, fog and storm.
I love to be with those I love.
I love to challenge myself.
I love to be happy when I'm finished even though I fail.
I went for a walk today, and the sun shone down,
the Earth shone up and
I shone in between, all one.

FROM ART WE CANNOT WANDER

From art we cannot wander.
Away from art we cannot dwell.
I dance, I draw, I write,
I carve, I sculpt, I knit, I sew --
    all in wonders' spell.

I share, I hide, I put myself asunder,
For though there is no art without me,
nor no art without us all.
We are art. We create the wonder
    each within our narrow selves.
But with our selves together
the infinite is spoken, drawn, and shared as art, as experience,
elusive, loving, mysterious as amongst ourselves.

IN A CEMETERY COMES

In a cemetery comes
the revelation that when I die
I am to be buried in the soil
in a shroud of my own making
to rot back to the inevitable wonder
that I am who I am.

CONVERSATIONS WITH DONALD HALL AND BOB DYLAN

So I'm reading the new
book of poems by Donald
Hall.
I stumble into an avalanche
of sound and rhythm,
familiar —

just a venture into the high country turned serious: how
a book of bared gravel voice and tumbling notes pushes raw
time down slopes I clawed up once or twice myself; how
I love that sweet music of conversation storied
on the solid pledge of truth in front of a fire
about the Dallas Cowboys interruptus,
some cattle loose in the road,
midnight neighbors in the cold front yard —
rolled out like an opera in a sometimes slight falsetto.
All the while listening to Bob Dylan's new CD
making fresh tracks with a grizzled dignity,
all honky-tonk guitar and voice of Spanish Leather
making diamonds still beneath an ocean of darkest night,
all jacked up in meaning disguised, or maybe no meaning at all —
gizzy-wigged like the opera in a sometimes slight falsetto.

So I'm warmin' me doze in front of the fire with Donald and Bob
and Lord, of a sudden I'm swept away like Scrooge,
three decades Christmas Past in Italy on me personal Via Dolce

somewhere between Munchen and Nizza:
Paperback Don and groovin' vinyl Bob a-backpack in the trunk while
the Hoosier haythatch hitchhike rider, I's
a-barreling down a cold Italian highway, radio-blastin' Citroën loge
floating opera in amongst three Mustachio'd Neapolitan topcoated,
bandied hatted, and pinkie ring-ed' floating hydropneumatic operatic
trio somewhere between tenor and basso;
who's driving? A moment, a conversation
with three generations of international Puccini fans
passing a hip flask singing unabashed raising hell and swelling
voices in a bold patrician, sometime slight falsetto.

BASTILLE DAY

She read to him as he sipped the freshly brewed tea. She had no compassion for his paralysis but enjoyed reading to herself and to others as well. Her voice was her compliment to the unknown gods who had created her miraculous body. There should be rewards for honest creation; the more honest, the more beautiful: the higher the reward. The gods — hers, at least — were overwhelmed with gratitude for this delicious specimen.

His sucking lips on the paper straw now being softened and disintegrated by the hot liquid pleaded with the tea not to be too hot, but to no avail. His lips burned, but he could not articulate his discomfort nor disengage the straw lest he disturb the polish on the last paragraphs she was reading and on those to come. There was no discomfort after the tea had passed his lips anyway. His face was all that he could willfully move or feel. Even his tongue was useless. He had to be told that he was choking when, as it sometimes happened, his instincts were confounded by his unruly brain. He silently pulled the straw further into his mouth.

The terrace on which they were seated faced the Mediterranean. The hot July sun was swathing their bodies in some of the most expensive light on earth. Once an hour she would turn him over in the chaise lounge with the machines attached, and since the paralysis had been getting on comfortably since February, both their bodies had achieved a coverage of blackness that only a completely idle Caucasian can aspire to. Their conversion evidenced a total revulsion for world of work or any form of labor.

She was nearing the end of her recitation. Could the skies have opened or the sun shone a little brighter as she finished? And now that he smiled in appreciation, his last mouthful of tea broke through the gaps in his teeth and dripped off his lower lip. Since he was fed intravenously, there was little joy in watching him slowly pass out with dehydration, so she went through the ritual of giving him something to drink so she could laugh at his mad antics. Her laugh was so delicious, she enjoyed it nearly as much as he, even though he only belatedly got the gist of most of her jokes – at his expense – because of his numb paralysis. It was all the delight – the Med, the sun, the sky and she.

Ah, yes, she moved with an easy grace, her fluid movements the only punctuation in his static picture of the blank and blue horizon, the straight top of the white terrace wall and the geometric simplicity of the terra cotta floor. She permitted nothing else. He faced the south and had at that a rather Gaullic view of it, red, white, blue, and all. Unexpectedly, she rose and faced him.

"Do you love me, darling?" she whined. "I never wish to seem imploring, but you haven't told me that you love me for some time." She burst out laughing. He returned her humor with a warm smile, as close to a laugh as he could come. He had a keen sense of humor, of course, and yes, he could not help but express his breathless appreciation of her human perfection.

"It's time for your afternoon feeding, darling; afterward I have a bit of a surprise for you." She set up the apparatus and plugged the IV bottle into the tube coming from his arm. "Down the hatch!" Ha, ha, the joy and wonder!

At that moment the catheter connected to his internals filled and he began voiding into a bag at the side of the chaise a somewhat disgusting but pitifully natural mixture.

"Where are your manners today, my man?" She pushed his head forward so that he could see the text of her gibe. She laid back his head and his eyes twinkled. His involuntary jokes pleased him most. What a glorious day!

"Do you know what day it is today?" This was a common joke between them, an affair entre deux. She had neither let him read nor observe any bit of printed material since the paralysis began. Day and night were spent in the same chaise in the same place. He had no indication other than the weather even what month it was.

"Today is Bastille Day. This evening we are to watch the fireworks from the village. We shall be inspired this evening." How clever she was, how amusing!

When it was nearly dark, she put a pillow behind his head so that he could glance down at his body and at the same time see over the terrace wall. She began purposefully massaging the body he could not feel and yet could see, and thus began to arouse the obvious simultaneous signals in his brain and disconnected bodily nerve ends.

His face began to flush as she manipulated herself before him. As he watched his body respond, he felt a warmth and fullness in his head. She began to breathe more deeply and for no other reason than that, so did he. She manipulated them both more excitedly until just before she was ready. She placed herself upon him, just as the fireworks from the village below began with a burst of color in his eyes. The fireworks increased in intensity and shone from her luminous skin. She climaxed collapsing forward on his uncontrolled and trembling body.

The rush continued in the sky, as he closed his eyes and felt an immense and overwhelming warmth deep behind them. His face related the colors of the bursting sky tingeing his skin with the subtle, prismatic play of artificial light.

At that moment she may have shot him square between the eyes and laughed.

LOCK IT UP!

There is no one more powerful than thee,
For regardless how you exit or explain
Unless you put lights out and lock up with a key,
Art work, yours or others' shared, may not remain.

Wicked Phantoms, Cats, or Lion Kings
May leave you Something Rotten in your dreams;
J. Whitcomb Riley will rhyme other horrid things
Unless you lock, front and back, "along the seams."

It's our shared treasure after all,
This wonder, our galleried Arts Association hall.

POOR ME (ALWAYS WORKING)

Ideas, yes, but working poems built on thoughts like these
often lead to revelations, meant to enlighten, not to please

(c'mon, dude, of course your sucking loneliness wants acknowledgement.
"not to please", ha! but still to churn, not to enter the establishment,
to help to realize the source of missing clatter
sifting through our poor brain, reflecting sleepless chatter
reflecting innocence but just the same
depth perceived from what I acknowledge is a shallow shame.
Poor me. They, they, the others
always over-gifted by we, have got it all
and now, poor me, I haven't -- or have I? -- yet collected attention
    -- here I am, after all --
that I, poor me, have to bear and bear and get nothing back
but words, attacks, seeming endless empty hangers on a rack.)

DOWNTOWN

I sit in the shade at a dark counter behind the glass,
eating my biscotti, sipping the dark, French roast
while drinking in the morning's entertainment out on the street.

Passersby are downtowners or touring souls or both;
some smoking on break or waiting for the play to begin
or beginning to play sidewalk music for sympathy or fee;
or sitting cross-legged with homeless sign and jar or not.
Walkers on a phone or and/or purple hair, tight braids,
cornrows, shaved mohawk or just brushed straight up,
low-hanging jeans falling off or threatening,
maybe a tie and skinny suit, panted or skirted,
crawling about with the crew at noon.

Baseball hats cocked on sideways, always more interesting
than backwards, cover inquisitive minds, bent on friends or girls
or hatless, just bent to laugh and explore, like me.

Here come the tie-less, open collared
point-shiny brown-shod or too-spike heeled,
conference-necklaced laughs and wondering
I suppose, like me, where desire will lead tonight.

RORRIM

He looks back at me,
reflects my order
to stop smiling and
not to stop because of him.
He asks to try a frown, to look into his eyes,
to wonder whether he is just the man he wants to be.
A movement here, ... and there, his eyes become
irresistible and wonder spreads from there.
Is this a simple morning in the mirror, or is it unbecome --
to see this being's gravity resisted by no one?

CARS, TRUCKS AND REBEL FLAGS

I think that I shall never see
more ignorance, rediculosity,
combined in Nazi-like complicity
than Rebel colors flagged on license-plated Rams 'n' F350z or planted
    front-porch, perhaps alongside a Trumper 2020

FEEDING INSTRUCTIONS

1. Find the key under the pot on the wicker table and enter through French doors in the atrium in the back of the house. …

2. Greet Bessie with a treat. Your choice. You'll learn. Put a couple in your pocket … or if you don't want your change to smell like bacon …

7. Although we walk her without the leash, Bessie demands attention and "range awareness." If she senses she is out of your domain, she runs around trying to find a new pile of deer pellets, a fresh road kill, or will sometimes chase the phantom beast into the woods. You know the phantom beast is around when she perks up, poses, and jerks her head from one pose to another. (She is beautiful when the phantom beast shows up, but she also uses it as an excuse to go her own way, indefinitely, and you are being paid by the trip rather than by the hour.) …

16. … Let Bessie escort you to the rabbit hutch.

17. At this point, depending on her appetite, Bessie will try to gulp down some rabbit goodies under the rabbit cage. She wouldn't be a dog otherwise. (Just a word of warning in case she tries to lick you later.) Make sure she uses her napkin. …

18. Change the rabbit water bottle and refill the food dish in the hutch. Access is through the small roof panel. …

20. Buster is the older of the two rabbits, white and now dominated by the other one, for whom, admittedly, we do not have the same feelings as those for Buster. Say "Hey, Buster," putting the right intonation on it and letting her know you know she is the victim of circumstance, a prisoner of her pink skin and eyes, her white fur, and the needs of the once weak and pitiful foundling rabbit who has matured to become a dominatrix at poor Buster's expense. The echoes of that greeting should indicate that Sadya, Vane and Randy will take her out more often, hold her, and let her walk on the fresh grass at every opportunity. And that she is a vivacious looking hunk of rabbit for a 10 year old. "Hey, Buster."

21. Walk Bessie till she has peed and pooped. We use the time-worn, "Make your BM, Bessie," because it does seem to have a salutatory effect. She will decide on a spot by a certain, almost telepathic movement, and will circle an extraordinary (seems to me, anyway) number of times. If the number is particularly high or if she changes

directions more than once, she does not take offense if you laugh. She is more than a dog.

22. … walk Bessie into the woods. (Because the threat of the phantom beast sometimes looms, and though some, among them I, prefer the gentle light of stars, regardless, the light switch for the outdoor lights is above the telephone, next to the French doors as you go out. They illuminate the rabbit hutch and the woods trail enough, in most cases, to foil the beast.) …

25. Release Bessie and spend as much time as you like smoking cigars, shooting darts, and otherwise socializing with her. …

27. Ah. Now Barney. Upstairs (through the living room from the kitchen bearing right, u-turn up, at the top, right.) in Sadya's playroom is the we-call-it terrarium with a chamelion in it. He hides in the lip of the cover sometimes, so be careful when removing it or he will be CRUSHED or ESCAPE! You probably won't have to remove the lid, though, because he has just been left 24 large crickets in a large leaf of lettuce. Crickets are living in Eden. Barney is on safari there. …

28. Spray the back side of the tank liberally with water [rain forest!] from the sprayer next to the we-call-it aquarium, but try not to hit Barney. He springs alarmingly fast and might hurt his delicate being.

29. … Say your goodbyes. Check the door to the basement once more and leave through the French doors. Rattle them to be sure they are locked.

TALKING TO MYSELF

When you read her note ...
at the second mention of depression alerted by the first,
leaving in a vacuum, your heart deserted,
somehow fluttered in the emptiness,
and echoed hollow chill inside this place you think.

Your face is cool, your breath is gone.
Along the path your longing (yes, it's longing) exposes some bare
truth --
like a single tuft of moss and lichen,
joyous color in a frozen winter wood --
so you see you see. You see you see?
Oh, you are so alone, without her, heartless,
yet breathing here amongst your fellows.

THE SHADOW OF THE OBJECT FALLING ON THE EGO

Master, is this why
I am mirrored in your eyes
Or wanting it so?

That reflection seen, do I go
with diagnosis, surprise,
excuse or goodbyes?

THE BUS

Through your kitchen window, you see your neighbor,
the asphalt seal-coater, driving his truck and trailer
up the gray winter street. Why is the roof-vent on the trailer open?
Full of asphalt, fumes and heat, the vent delivers me dreams.

The big, yellow bus emerges beneath you as you saw an opening for the
vent soon to come in its roof.

You experience clear, eucalyptus air and laughter as your father helps
below in the California clarity where you and wife have parked the bus
of dreams.

The bus wouldn't fit on the neat steep curvy street
where your father lives in the beautiful hillside house
with the deck, the flowers, tiny green front yard, his crumbling marriage
suburbanized across the Golden Gate.

Lying back in the beanbag chair on astroturf in your bussing living
room,
stopped en route anywhere -- in the desert, on the shore, among the
Tetons --
vent lids, screens and cranks float above in ceiling-painted rainbow.

You look down again while sawing, see your dad's white hair and
moustache in front of his smile, then debussed-decades later turn to
awake in today's gray morning, longing all.

Now through your kitchen window, you see your neighbor, the asphalt
seal-coater driving his truck with the heavy black trailer, go up the gray
winter street. The roof-vent on the trailer is open. You wonder why it's
open on this subfreezing day: is the trailer full of questions? of heat?

As he passes, you find yourself through another window, sitting atop
the big, yellow bus while you saw an opening to fit one of its roof vents.
You sense your father helping below, inside, though you cannot see him;
you experience clear, leafy air and laughter in the suburban clarity of the

California street where you have parked the bus en route across America to see everyone and -place you know and never did.

The bus you learned to drive on and off the ferry from Alaska, through Seattle, across the Columbia, the Oregon coast, down the Pacific Coast Highway. Here you are in Marin, a lifestyle mecca where there is temporary rest, family and obligation.

You could not park to fit the bus on the steep side over the hill along a curvy, neat street where your father lives in a house carved into the rock with his crumbling marriage, deck, flowers, tiny watered green front yard, so you parked it here.

One morning you twice cut square openings in the yellow, rounded oof. You cut on through the ceiling and a band of color in the rainbow painted in Alaska. You accidentally cut a knot of wires between those two metal sheets sandwiching '50s insulation and Detroit engineering, and thus learned vehicular electicity from the simple teacher, Accident. You see the roof vents' close-up workings -- screens and cranks and moving air -- and you, sprawled in the beanbag chair on astroturf beneath the painted rainbow, stopped somewhere en route to nap. You miss the kitty and Jacquie sitting in the stuffed chair next to you as you drive.

Looking down again through a finished vent opening, you see your dad's white hair and moustache in front of his smile, then return to writing in the gray morning as the neighbor's trailer with its mysterious vent emerges from the sparkling mist of the yellow bus, leaking inspiration.

GRAVITY

Gravity, whose ... mysterious attraction
creates a physics ignored.

Love, the gravity irresistible, drawing us to touch;
Love, drawing me to your anahata;
Love, the source of mysterious, yet inevitable energy;
Love, that gives, yet takes my breath away;
Gravity, the inevitable and irresistible mystery of you.

ALEXANDER TECHNIQUE

Walked past, by your place today,
in the neighborhood, you know, after scouting poetry
at a bum academic show of a score of miserable poets' ego.
I looked up at your gently glowing windows
in whose light you work and share your art, expecting nothing.

At the outdoor market once, where we agreed to meet, expecting street
    domestic garb, I looked, explored and couldn't find you; but then,

Your beauty wrapped in personally glamorous dress
and elegant style shone out, not of vanity, but care.
One evening in that light I witnessed your artistic being amongst
those who share your practice who shared
their talent, music, movement, and delighted in your voice.
We kissed in a soft romance several evenings there,
chatted, shared, explored --
even learned to float a perfect soft-boiled egg on water --
respectful admiring and parting, each to dream alone.
One evening, as I saw you wave good night
from that perfect windowlight, I blew you a kiss,
neither desiring nor expecting it would be my last.

GOLF

The objective of most golf shots is to move the ball as far as it will go from
its present position directly toward the cup. This notion creates one of golf's
greatest attractions to players at all levels: on any given shot, a novice golfer
can hit a shot whose result is as good as that of any professional in the sport.

Even though a novice may perform as well as a professional on any given
shot, most golfers are concerned with game of golf – being able to make
every shot as good as it can be, to score well consistently, and to learn
about oneself and life along the way.

Like many things, success in golf is actually very simple. By learning and
following a few simple, universal rules consistently, the fun and depth of
golf emerge.

Be Here Now.

A golf shot has no past. No matter how the ball arrived where it lies, the ball and target are where they are for each shot, now. Each golf shot is a solution to a new problem: getting the ball from where it is now to the target.

Direction is Power

The ball and the target create a line. The line creates direction. The closer you come to hitting on that line, the better the shot will be. The better each shot is, the better your score. There is no such thing as a great golf shot in the wrong direction. A shot close to the line with the right club will always produce a good result.

Distance will take care of itself.

The club determines distance. A consistent, focused, full swing with the right club – from the driver to the sand wedge – is the most common type of golf shot. According to the rules of golf, a player may have up to 14 golf clubs in a set. Each club is designed to hit the ball at a different angle or loft. Except for the putter (and some other specialized clubs you don't need), the greater the angle of the face of the club relative to the ground, the shorter the shot. By varying the loft, you vary the distance the ball can travel.

Half the shots are putts.

'Par' in golf means taking two putts on every green in addition to the one, two or three shots to get to the green. In eighteen holes of golf, par expects you to have 36 putts. Play on and around the green most often determines the score. Chipping and putting consistently are as important to the game as are the shots from the tee and fairway. Direction and distance are even more important around the green than they are in the long game.

Remember: Be here now. Direction is power. Distance will take care of itself. Half the shots are putts.

Going in the right direction

A golf shot is described conventionally as consisting of The Address and The Swing. Trying to break down and recombine the components of a shot is very complex. The split second between the address and the swing makes an obvious division point.

The Address/Swing shot process was described most simply and profoundly by the respected American statesman and philosopher, Davy Crockett, who said, "Be sure you're right, and then go ahead."

Address

The goal of the address is to create the exact circumstance in whichyou are relaxed, comfortable and ready to swing.

During the address you go through a personal checklist. Generally, themore automatic and familiar it becomes, the better. After choosing theclub, based on the distance and circumstances sand trap, putting green,and so on of the shot.

Get comfortable. Be in the present. Focus on the ball and your target.

Create your stance.

1. Set the club behind the ball in such a way that its base is sitting naturally flat on the ground and perpendicular to the line of the shot. "Perpendicular" means that you always set it on the line at a consistent angle so you are confident that it is a point of reference.
2. Get a soft grip. Let the club sit in the position and grip the shaft without changing the relationship of the club to the ball. We'll cover the grip later.
3. Create a line with the tips of your toes that parallels the line created by the ball and the target. Rotate around the ball and club to get this line rather than setting the feet first.

This toeline is important is because it becomes your base reference for all shots made on level ground with no obstacles regardless of the club you use.

In some instances you will vary the stance, but always in reference to this line.

For instance, if you are on a slope, you align your feet differently to control the shot, but one or the other of the toes will always be positioned on this imaginary line, pointing at the target.

The distance you stand away from the ball is dynamic because it changes with the club, the grip, and the position of your feet. The initial alignment of your feet, though, is consistent.

Your weight should wind up being evenly distributed between and slightly forward on the balls of your feet, but never on your toes.

Get a Grip
1. I use the classic overlapping grip, which means that your left forefinger overlaps the right little finger, and the knuckles of both hands form a straight line down the club.
2. The left thumb fits in the valley between the thumb pad and the heel of the right hand.
3. The V of the left hand points to the right shoulder.
4. The club should be in the fingers of the right hand and the palm of the left hand.

Vary your stance, grip, and swing to control direction.
Remember: direction is power. Distance takes care of itself.

If you've had a few lessons or have read much about golf, you already know most of what I've said. But the game is all about reference fundamentals. Just like in any sport the best players always understand the fundamentals and continue to hone them. A natural player is someone who has played a lot.

SWING
The swing begins with your head and the ball.

1. Your head is always the same distance from the ball throughout the swing, until you hit the ball.
2. Your arms and the club stay within a narrow plane around your center of rotation as you swing. I think of my arms and club as swinging inside a pizza box suspended around my neck.
3. The swing is smooth, fluid arid continuous, first in the back swing to store energy and then in the fore swing to release the energy at the point of contact with the ball until the ball leaves the club head.
4. The center of rotation is your spine. It is suspended by your thorax, hips, legs, and ultimately by your feet. Your arms, shoulders, thorax,

hips, and legs all rotate around the spine to produce the power of the swing. I use the mental picture of my spine as a kinetic reference for my swing.

5. The swing is focused on the ball. The hardest part of a swing is forgetting about its components during execution so that the rotation of the legs, hips, shoulders, arms, hands, and club becomes a smooth transition from storing energy through translating it through the ball.

The line to the target, stance, grip, club position, and distance have all been absorbed when the swing begins. Give over the mechanics of execution to the lower brain and body (which, remember, can be trusted even while you're unconscious), focus your conscious mind on the ball, relax, and swing.

6. Keep your head still

Once the swing is established, the most common adjustment is to the plane of the swing. The way it works seems counter intuitive.

The more horizontal the plane of the swing, the more you tend to hook.

The more vertical the plane of the swing, the more you tend to slice.

Hooking and slicing.
To straighten out a hook
- reference check the swing
- swing more slowly and rhythmically
- change the plane of the swing from inside out to outside in
- reference check the stance
- keep the right toe on the line and move the left foot back
- reference check the grip
- roll the right hand over the left, more over the shaft of the club.

To straighten out a slice
- reference check the swing
- swing more slowly and rhythmically
- change the plane of the swing from outside in to inside out
- reference check the stance

- keep the left toe on the line and move the right foot back
- reference check the grip
- roll the right hand back off the left, more behind the club.

YOU WIN.

WORLD NEWS TONIGHT (2002)

The day darkened blue grey and poured down
rain on the world earlier today.
Grass grew under the wet heat
and the cool sweet rush of air before
the lightning shook the trees in thunder.
More rain is expected tomorrow and tomorrow.

Last week's storm exploded the bark from
a respected, two-hundred-year-old walnut
and blew the ground up off its roots.
Though reported critical, it seemed to have survived —
counting its decades more patiently than most —
but during the week it weeped off young leaf clusters
in a slow, uncontrollable rhythm, barely perceptible.

The grosbeaks come to join the singers and peckers,
the bullies, the meek, and other proud birds at the feeder.
A single thrush ate and trilled, delighting onlookers
while the old man who grooms her left clumps of Bessie's
black hair on the low garden wall near the house.

People in the house are studying for final exams,
the Prom at the Plaza, and the deepening, anxious sadness
of parents' imprudent end-games.

The May flies are gone, but throngs of mosquitos
emerge from standing water, roam the heavy air
and suck life out of unwitting hosts. Dozens have been killed in
    continuing hand to hand personal violence
while others are simply chased down and disappeared
by roaming gangs of bats and swallows.

Locusts bloomed and dropped their supple yellow flowers
in two short days a couple of weeks ago. Yesterday
their primordial green leaf fronds sifted leisurely
shadows from the light of the late afternoon.

Bessie had a bloody, near-death spell of
diarrhea and vomiting last evening,
woke her alpha at 3:06 am after a guilt-ridden dream
of fighting excrement on a despairing, humid day.
She hunched and stumbled about outside,
poured out the remainder of her bowels and wretched
a neat pile of curds in the darkness. She's still a dog.

The alpha ran his hand under the blown off bark shroud still hanging
    fresh on the walnut and was stunned to experience the electric thrill
of its smooth, damp cambium and expressed his pleasure in the tips of
    broken capillaries looking like freckles
on its exposed supple flesh in the quiet morning light.

By afternoon the clear and wondrous luster of its lifeblood had turned
    wet black.

AM I DAVID?

Surrounded by quiet circumstance and days-long isolation --
the vacationing Poets' gift --
I walk naked freely, alone, atop the mossy rocks,
among the massive trees and off-spring,
along the steeply nestled creek to dip in the pool
above an old log dam wedged between the banks.

Along the dog-worn trail passing a fire circle and a labyrinth of rock,
back to the exquisitely purposeful yet seeming random-built and
    scattered house,

embedded safe and secure in the mountain over years,
I pass berries, leaves, flowers, plantings and fruits of the endless garden,
enter through the spacious, airy, well-appointed vacationing dogs'
    apartment (some would say, "enclosed bare-wood porch").

Back inevitably to the Poets' den of intellectivity:
rare and rarefied, addictive library corners, enchanting shelves of
    collections,
Camus, Rodin, Baudelaire, Dickinson, Michelangelo, Dylan,
fireplace, piano, guitar, commentary, candles and plants.

Still naked, and but for my paradisiacal isolation's looming Goliath the
    voice who threatens me with return to the human world from this
    nest in paradise I watch, asking my reflection in every mirror and
    glass for courage and a sling,
"Are you David?"

for Mary and Heller

WHERE AM I?

Where am I?
Like, yeah, no, like becoming some first times.
You know, uh,
You know the inadequacy, our shared experience,
where you, like, know what you want, yeah, no,
and I know, too.
You, a mystery, infusing me with nuclear fuel,
like Iran, illegal according to some,
but so powerful to us locals, so legal, so impossible to deny.

BIG BANG

Train track, heavy ride, out the window seated
on the railroad from the Center of the World
to the City of Brotherly Love.
We share recent gifts of the industrial age, unwrapped:
Quonset hut, fac-to-ry re-painted blue, second
generation windows re-viewed with cement block and
welded iron, thoughts in artificial light between the bars.
Tanks woven in a chemical warp of pipe,
"Machine Shop" "Print Shop" "PVC" shuttle between
cast off spikes and monger's twisted iron delights,
"Deli" steak and cheese.
Walkups, fire escapes porched in; I doze of walking
down this cinder alley track-bed home-to-work and back,
waving engineer, neighborhood sleep in motion:
yards, houses, streets and rails, sidewalk lullabyways leading from my
    roiling bed.
Elemental rhythms beat in bare cement and rusting iron,
smokey stone and mud, in slave and master,
loll me deep adream, tuned to wasted smells of pleasure and astral
    hymns of ribonucleic religion.
The Mysteries of the painted glass panes
broken here and there in symmetric rusted frames,
the big bang and inherent gravity of life
twist amongst the sticks and bones, the dark matter,
the hieroglyphs on pyramids, ruined satellites and parthenons in
    this train on the way from the Center of the World to the City of
    Brotherly Love.

RIVER OF LOVE

A river of love flows
out of my heart
non-stop. And another out of yours.

Our torrential flood
flows into the frail human desert
surrounding us,
willing to sustain life in abundance and
the thirst for keeps.

Yet here is sand,
And elusive aboriginal arts aside,
I see no silk and spice in caravan,
no oasis, beyond the slippery banks
of this lonely violent flood.

February 9, 1999

SEVENTH WAVE

Stunned, not swept off my feet,
my feeling, inadequate,
somehow absorbs the love for you that comes
to break, warm, around and then within me.
It is not a constant, burning heat,
not lapping sweet nor massive crest tsunami.
But like the rhythm of the seventh wave,
almost inevitable, it breaks and, more than expectation,
more than passing, overwhelms.

1/1/2014

I TOOK A WALK TODAY

I took a walk today down by the falls, in sunshine along the railroad
I tightroped the tracks and timed the ties to step along the day.
I took a walk today, by my magnificent river, under full moon and stars,
I reason an excuse for tides, for bridges, ferries, docks and parks.
I took a walk today to open up my spirit, to give me time.

Time to fly, time to recognize my ignorance,
Time to open up myself to all my possibilities,
Time to stop thinking of them and every detail in between.

I love where I am because it is where I am.
I love to watch, to look, to have this Earth around me.
I love to walk in sunshine, rain, fog and storm.
I love to be with those I love.
I love to challenge myself.
I love to be happy when I'm finished even though I fail.

I took a walk today and the sun shone down, the Earth shone up and
I shone in between, all one.

June 7, 2015

BOOKTALK

Thank you for joining in this journey with me. Do you hate it when someone calls some simple pencil scratches on paper accelerated into a book, a journey? But proceeding in the spirit, not having had a drop yet, by the way, ['by … the way', get it?] I am glad you are willing to share the toll on the road to the end.

It keeps me alive.

If I didn't think you were there to pay the freight so to speak, had something in your pocket there on the seat beside me, that is, to buy some grub and have some left over on the other end of the turn-pike [page-turn pike – do I have to explicate?], I would just quit.

Like you and the rest of us faced with pressing ahead, I mean moving forward, not pressing per se, but then again ['then again', think about it: I'm trying not to repeat myself and besides, you get in beside me here on this journey, taking a seat that you paid for once again, you get my drift; 'you get my drift', think about it]

I must be putting the pedal to the metal or you wouldn't have laid out the cost of the ride already.

You know you're hitchhiking, and I'm hoping you have a beer or a story or a joint or a kindly place to rest if needs be; that is, my ride with you already beside me, my having something virtual to look forward to, by virtue of your having hopped in and having already gotten here [x], then I guess the ride-journey metaphor doesn't work quite, given that you could have picked up the book … stop me right here … you picked up a book that's already a book so's it must have already been paid for by somebody and then you might or might not put it down or bring it to the register, risking the guilt that you paid the toll or just had a cup of coffee and paid the toll to somebody else who already bought the book that you're willing, if you did bring it to the register, to gamble it be worth the ride, price, burden and the guilt over both the coffee and the coffee and the book when there's a baby, education, house, Mercedes in your drive, a future that may have benefited by not having been preempted by our journey begun here in front of us, since you got in.

So isn't it the truth, hard to be authentic here, stay on track [on a journey home or away, on the seat beside me in the car or train or ox cart box, maybe scanning the horizon] when cool cynicism put those last words down, needs be that there's a little bit of toll ready, maybe gas money, then I guess we're already on our way in a respectful sort of way, you acting your part and I acting mine [and, of course (course, heh) directing].

Just so you know where I'm coming from, so hard just to be here, inside the journey you could burn or close, I feel like I've already given too much of my gratis side and need to share my gravis side, as opposed to my graveside, since you already put your change on the table so to speak to read this.

You and a few thousand others, I hope.

Words are so easy to get on and ride.

2010

DANCER

Rare fortune to witness the wonder of a pair of vultures
cleaning bones of a dead fox on rocksy stage in deep wood
finding themselves discovered under the gaze of dogs and I.

As we approach the cliff the vultures rise in silence absolute
with the fundamental sacred beauty of their powers in air,
to float effortlessly up and above to wait for us to pass
having no sense of their wondrous beauty, their performance.
As much as the remains of the fox, we're simply witness to their
    innocent, inevitable being.

A witness to your beauty fills one with wonder and desire.
Without performance your every move and being dance,
inevitable being, inevitable dance.
"Touch me, dance, and let me trust you."

Music

Sacred dance extempo-rare, I dare
recall my strength, possessed to embrace your fair
swooping arc unbound, unbroke, rebound
to balance perfect time to perfect end, a dance woven into life.

At the window, in the street, as I breathe
Sudden dreams electric shudder chakrac isles
Shiver neck, envelope heart, course current wile
To quake desire, remembrance, embodied vision,
aftershock after shock, we dance.

AFTERMATH A MEMORY -- THE LOVERS

Birds goes
loosely wingen
through air silent reign
feather glide motion
gentle ocean
rain pliddle sand drops.
In dawn calm breathen rhythm mist
o'er we wet skin-foot-walken soft beach
hand in hand
the birds goes.

Leaves blows ...
soft piana-key-playen wind fingers
strum tuneful hush music smilen
summer-shaded forest downy
breath of lovers breathing.
When dark come warmen naked to kiss
close lyen open wet and touchen,
we watch stars back through black patches
the leaves blows.

Love knows
nuzzle open flowing
closeness gentle, warm in
whispered kissing moistness,
candid hands, possessive lips and
passion heaving percèd to the rooten
bodies now arose with petals licoured wetness
swollen hote to one the other melden
madly to-and-gether naked lovelay
soaken bursting inside one an other
one eternal molten ecstasy
only love knows.

IN THE WOODS

I saw in the paper that the moon would transit Saturn
on a particular night at about four in the morning.
I had a vision of the great ringed planet passing –
setting like a movie poster vision – slowly behind the moon.

This is my illusion.

Now I believe I walk beneath my stars.
I believe the moon is shining through my woods
and through limbs, Saturn and Jupiter, my friends.
The wind has ceased and smells are close,
as close as quiet in my woods now lit only by the moon.
My friends the dogs, oblivious to my quiet woods, my stars
and ages of needy, random reflection and misdirection
are my companions on this short journey, this illusion,
I believe, and share their own with me.

One New Years Eve not quite midnight I described to Elizabeth
the transit of Saturn by my moon on that peculiar night:
how the Great Ringed Ball of Gas empostered never appeared,
how the simple, planetary light and friend to dogs
passed irreconcilably behind the dark rim
of the mountains on the edge of the moon;
that the light reflected back, directly to my perfect eyes
had been created hours before in the energy of the sun
and spun off, there and back, and different light
on its own sweet time had spun my vision of the moon.

Beneath my stars, my moon whose edge
on the limbs where it rests is sharp,
I walk in the rhythm of my moon, the stars, my woods,
my moon, my illusion.

Inevitably this night reflected from Elizabeth's different light
now spins my limbs, my dogs, my moon itself,
the message, her message delivered toneless,
in transit of her shadowed despair.

Between 2001, 2002, some egg nog, and my vanity,
I ratcheted on ... how the moon and planets' motion
generate a personal sound
as the swirling silver gas and dusty rings,
reflecting light from the sun would
approach and disappear behind the limned moon --
my great and ringèd ball of gas
just a simple point of light, now there,
now not, disappearing, reappearing somewhere, ever.

Now reflecting this poor light on my friend
Elizabeth's quiet hopes last New Year's Eve,
comes this particular moon in these particular woods tonight
no less momentous than a disappearing point of light
or Elizabeth's realized despair
or my dark wander, pointless, here in the woods,
reflected to the open sky, with dogs and snow and failing sight
tangled amongst Great Gas Balls reflecting an invisible sun.

April 8, 2002

GRAVITY

I write in longhand.
I do not know what gravity is.
Something draws us together.
It is not deep within or enveloping us.
Nor is it out there.
This drawing together is our doing,
yet we do not know it at all.

Snow and ash falling together
and dust in air are simply distractions.
an energy, a physics unknown
draws us together, inseparable.

5/2008

VACUUM

I. If nothing exists, show it to me.
"1960s" not "1960's".
"us" not "u's".
"us" is not "us".
"us" is not "we".
Double u is in a vacuum
We are in a vacuum; w is not.
Is anybody out there?

II. I don't think we abhor nothing.
Is nothing a vacuum?
A vacuum contains nothing.
Nothing is a vacuum.
Nature abhors a vacuum.
Nature abhors nothing.
There is nothing in Nature that Nature abhors, because
Nature abhors nothing, least of all a vacuum.
Nature cannot abhor nothing, because nature can abhor nothing.
If Nature is everything, then everything is natural.
Nature contains nothing, so nothing is natural.
Nature does not contain everything if it does not contain itself.
Nature contains nothing, itself, and everything else.

III. Final Exam: Vacuum
Are the two us empty?
Does dead always come after death or
is there just "dead"?
There are dead things in Nature.
There are dead things in me. And you?
Does dead end and not alive begin?
Limestone: dead? Gold: dead? Nothing: dead? Us: dead?
Nothing is natural. Everything is natural.
Nothing is unnatural. Show me us.
Show me nothing. Show me everything unnatural.
Where does a vacuum end?

JOBHUNT

Begin life
  Loop forever
    select jobs
      from

            self
            mom & dad
            friendly suggestions
            school, church, grocery bulletin board
            internet job postings
            email postings
            want ads
            higher authority
                (god, wife, brother-in-law, boss,
                children)
      where
            better salary, calories, sex, love, music

      For each job
            create cover communication concept
            research resume concept files
            create/write cover communication
                (letter, email, painting, blocks, smile)
            attach resume
            customize resume
            copy package to file
            send to hiring authority

            if called for interview
                make two copies of resume and cover
                letter
                trim nose and ear hair
                dress like potential boss
                arrive early with resumes
                if offered job
                    compare with
                      current
                      shelter, income, location,

love
pending opportunities
discuss with
family
significant others
current god
if discussion results in
acceptance
add to resume
give acceptance
start work
bring home check and
benefits
end if accept job offer
end if job offer
end if interviewed
end each job
end select
end loop
end life
#20010903

A NIGHT YOU NEEDED ME

I lay with you last night
asking why I want I want I've wanted you, you, yes, you,
and yet my only comfort is to hold you, though I'm roused;
just to breathe in sync for hours while you sleep,
to think, to reminisce, to try to find my secret key
to your heart, my heart that now I realize is brass.

Your fox-rimmed, hooded leather costume mystifies me
till I walk behind you, your naughty womanhood,
costumed in a youth you do not need for me, for anyone:
your boots, your jeans, your darkened eyes
alluring to me and you, and yet so wanting wasted in allure.

You ask me only to be your friend, a friend, and I see it now:
I have never understood what I've had to offer you,
you've seldom asked, the you who's given me so much,
so selfless, timing perfect in its edgy way,
and now it turns to this sleepless night, parsing breath and silence
holding my beating heart to yours, your electric anahata,
breathing in, breathing out
until you finally sleep and breathe and sleep
baring my regrets, my endless negligence exposed, not just in dreams,
    my loss so obvious yet not to me till now.

HOW'S JACK?

How's Jack, I dream, I walk a-dazed,
I gather circumstance,
I gather courage to approach you,
one who said I wasn't who she thought.

I, aye, eye, am, is, are, tangled
in your special wonder.
The you who took me for
the ultimate lover, more, I thought, I guess,
but whose world extended far beyond
your realization, even though
you thought you knew,
the one you actualized every day;
the one with whom I traveled, never questioned, never asked
your special friends and places more than names.

Are you my Athena,
the one whose gifted silk and fashioned clothes I wear,
whose travel shared and with whom witnessed wonder, space,
the greatest city in the world, from another hemisphere,
yet with doggie Jack in your one-room gallaried art
living with a host who huddles darkened in her room,
in a constant, tv-lit cloud of weed?

No, you are your own no matter where. You are
the one I wanted and I the one
you imagined wanted you.
Too far away from wonderland
you fantasized us in a cloister,
and I imagined ecstasy there between us
measured in between your many paths.

Is anyone there who has yet better met your test?
Are you the object of my desire
and I of yours? In whom these words bring
out some electric spirit we both can share

Are you the one, electric magic paradise,
Or are you my electric chair?

CHIMERA

The twins, the other voices roaming free in my brain ...
My whole wholly personal family
telling me I'm perfect
telling me I'm an idiot
telling me to share
telling me I'm wrong
telling me I'm bad
telling me the way ...

so often telling.

CONNIE'SBIRTHADDRESS

Four score and eight years ago her parents brought forth on this continent a new humanist, conceived in liberty, and dedicated to the proposition that all men are created equal and deserve equal justice.

She has engaged in a great civil life, proving that she, or any person so conceived and so dedicated, can long endure. We are met at a familiar, nearby restaurant to celebrate her birth date and that life. We have come to celebrate a personal friend and universal wonder who has continued to bring dance, music, children, justice, joy, honor, peace and delight to a world of friends, family, causes, practices, WESPAC, The Connie Hogarth Center for Social Action at Manhattanville College and emails. It is altogether fitting and proper that we should do this.

But, in a larger sense, we can not dedicate, we can not consecrate, we can not hallow this person. Her brave, gentle and powerful life has consecrated it far above our poor power to add or detract. The world will little note, nor long remember what we say here, but it can never forget what she has accomplished here. It is for us, the dining, rather, to be here dedicated to the great task remaining before us -- that from her, our honored friend and spirit, we take increased devotion to the causes for which she continues giving her full measure of devotion -- that we here highly resolve that we friends, under whatever god, universe, humanist or spiritual belief, shall have a new birth of enthusiasm -- and that Connie Hogarth shall be celebrated forever.

November 19, 2014

FICTION

There is fiction, a lifelong fiction I created in spite of myself ...
love from a storybook created simply by desire, desire to satisfy,
desire to escape, desire to give another her idea of love
and inevitably to find the giving empty.
Then I desired you.

MOCKINGBIRD

The crow settles out of the grey-clouded sky
that frames a peaked shingled roof,
its brick chimney capped with tile.
Wings beat agentle twice, slowing, then lifting
so the feet spread a toe's width above the roof peak,
then settle as if there were no flight.
The crow stands, and with a shudder shakes the muscles out
then scouts the street and neighbors with quick, full-headed glances
    all around.

Across the street a mockingbird sits atop the tile atop its chimney
cheater cheater churning turning into female-stopping
sweet jagged rhythms and piercing cluster chords
that may even impress a crow
and certainly humiliate a poet trying awfully hard to learn his secret.

GIRL WITH A PEARL EARRING

Venus came to me poised on a shell emerging from the ocean, her eyes on mine, defining my definition of ultimate beauty from the artist's bookshelf where I re-acquainted my youthful self with her often.

An invitation and a need to bring our senses of self to each alone had brought us random to a shared promise of Buddhist enlightenment.

Don't know whether it worked, but we found promise. And fortunate was I to know just then alive the most beautiful woman in the world.

PARABOLIC CURVES

How I love telephone poles and wires in the fall. The mellowing browns and blacks are extraordinary. The looping, parabolic curves bring me to my knees. The cross bars, insulators, joint-boxes, transformers -- all

natural -- share my rapt attention. I barely see the no parking signs and streets of asphalt and cement. Somehow they represent life eternal while the trees and flowers discolor, die and fall behind them, barely noticed.

SUBURBAN THERAPY

I want to start a new life. Before the day is out I must change my habits, everything I can, my point of view…

David Rabe, *Recital of the Dog*

As usual, I am just late for a train, the 8:53, headed for the city. Obviously the 8:53 is already late. By the time the 8:53 spews its contents out in the city, the gears of the great financial, processing, and communications machines have already been turning for hours.

The 8:53 is for those who are just-in-time; mostly lawyers and consultants paid simply to clean up the mess or provide entertainment after the real business has been done. Or those who are relaxed, retired, expired. Or on their way to an interview full of hope. Or on their way to a play. But if I were on the 7:53, I wouldn't be just-in-time. Others would be.

Here I am in my dark, stylish suit, one suit in a collection of grizzly $1200 corporate overalls on hangers in my closet. Today I have worn my favorite. It blends a secret need for a somewhat personal style and a need to conform just enough – with the expectations of those who paid to watch me perform. I am on my way to an 11:30 presentation, purportedly to report the truth and light the way for a company entering the big time.

In the spirit of my expertise in just-in-time systems, I just finished putting together the presentation just a little over five hours ago and got just enough sleep. As expected, it turned out just great.

And now I have dallied another 20 minutes and missed even the 8:53. I'm late. Now it's the 9:27. Now I am racing for the 9:27 at my closest stop. As I cross the tracks in my just old enough Subaru, I see the headlights of the 9:27 flowing downtrack toward the station. Parking and making the train at the station is thus out of the bounds of reality, absurd. I can't park within 500 yards, and even if I ran to the platform at world class, 400m time … forget it.

But I am compelled to make that train. Otherwise I won't make it at all to that roomful of expectant, downsized, just fine guys and a gal. If I make a mad run at it and all goes perfectly, I can still just make that train. I wheel around, pass back over the tracks and head down the line for the next station. But when I get to the next station, same story. Train looms, no real parking within miles. But I realize that if I head for the stop after next, I gain an extra seven minutes, the scheduled difference in the time between the stations. And parking. I can simply risk getting a twenty-dollar ticket for overtime parking in the two-hour slots in the station lot, since I'll be parked the whole day.

And I have a shot at getting a break on the ticket. The traffic wardens for that lot have sometimes overlooked my old Subaru in a two-hour slot with an expired meter. On occasion I've even gone to the trouble of creating a tableau for them: the slightly dusty, red Subaru, the windows down and a Times on the seat. The "just a local guy gone in for a cup of coffee" tableau.

I race for the on-ramp to the Parkway. I just make every light and hit the entrance ramp smoothly with no stops. When I pull off the Parkway, the light is … just right. I know I have beaten the train two stops, but unless all goes well with the meters and the parking, I will still pay twenty dollars for humiliation if I get a ticket and my wife finds out. If I get the ticket and hide it, I will really feel like a deadbeat. Then again, if I pay it promptly, she won't even see it, but it will fester into a self-inflicted humiliation of guilty silence.

My self-righteous mate has me by the throat in the traffic department. I speed. I forget my seatbelt. I phone and text. I have a "Denali" insurance payment … because. She who forgets she nearly killed herself recently because she just looked down to tune her radio while driving too close, too fast in a line of cars through a curve, plowed into the back of the car in front of her, and totaled her car. Of course, in her interpretation, it wasn't her fault; it was the nut who u-turned out of sight around the curve who caused the line to stop in awe.

She is on my case, fortified by our insurance bills and the points against my license when she picks up the mail and pays the bills. It doesn't stop though I'm a safe driver who just drives too fast.

Left turn off the ramp, in a zone of awareness, totally paranoid about speeding (for total paranoia is total awareness), I race at double the speed limit the last half-mile down a commercial street and just make the second light, then accelerate around the curve – Sweet! This Subaru handles like a Lola – up toward the hill, the other side of which is the last light. Brake lights are going off in the line of cars beginning to move up the hill ahead! The light over the hill must've just turned green! Cresting the hill I see it turning back to yellow, but I just make it turning left over the tracks beneath the railroad station bridge. From the bridge I take a quick glance up the tracks – no train – then swing right too fast through the station lot and right and right again into the parking lot between the station and the strip mall across the street.

The train hasn't whistled, but the "half past" bells are ringing from the church nearby. Could I have beaten the train by a full four minutes? The bells can be off by several minutes either way, but I drive on past the line of sure thing, open two-hour slots into the single lane of earlybird, eight hour meters. I feel it, a small disturbance that hints to go ahead. The odds are highly against my finding an open eight hour slot, but I can make up the time if there isn't one. I'll bypass the station and go straight to the platform. Rather than go into the station, I'll pay an extra five dollars for a ticket on the train – a bargain to eliminate the potential of humiliation.

And to the left, as if delivered on a divine wind, there appears a single, open eight hour slot. And a roll of quarters in the tray in front of me! Eight hours! Instead of losing, I have gained back all lost time and more. I park, grab the briefcase, lock the car, feed the quarters into the meter, and carelessly lope the short remaining distance to the station door. Still no train as I dance into the station! I am still running, but I have won.
I take another 30 seconds to buy a Times to read on the train. The presentation on acetate is all ready, and even now I have almost an hour slack in the city before I present it anyway. I get off-peak tickets down and back – I wouldn't have gotten off-peak rates even on the 8:53 – and blow out the track door. Long strides to the stairs. Then up the stairs to the pedestrian bridge over the northbound track two stairs at a time. Looking up the tracks to the window on the bridge over the platform, the train is slowing for the station. Down the stairs from the bridge, onto the platform trackside, catch a breath. Just in time.

The train slows to a stop as I do. The conductor waits for the exact time, 9:34; the doors open, and I step aboard. Cosmic.

I sense the net of capillaries within the uppermost layer near the sensory surface of the skin flowing with oxygen, nutrients, and exquisite, molecular messages. Each hair stands in its swollen, fleshy pore over a sweat-filled gland, each one primed to refresh my skin and ruin the starch in my shirt. But the cool air of the car is just cool enough to cool me just enough, just with air. No sweat.

Into the standing area on the entryway aisle between the doors on either side of the car, I am about caught up with breathing. I am groomed by the air. I am filled with a victorious, hormonal essence. I am practically floating. My perception is heightened by the strange mix of air and adrenaline. And the most beautiful woman on the train is waiting – an empty seat beside her.

Ecce homo. I take the seat.

A VISION

We lie naked face to face in semidarkness,
your body's profile an exquisite, timeless curve ...

We touch, explore each other gently, somehow not erotic, looking,
seeing, exposing to each other
a wonder that is eternal, yes, erotic, yes, ours alone.

I DON'T KNOW

Once I asked a new friend, "How old are you?"
She answered appropriately, "I don't know."

At a 50th anniversary reunion,
I fell in love with a bunch of old people
with whom I had fallen in love many times before,
each time a wonder, each time anew,
each one unique, each a surprise,
each one so deep I never knew.
I'm astonished, in awe, in a stew:
how can I love, how renew,
how can I thank, how can I be in love so much
with you and you and you?
Brothers and sisters, lovers and friends,
I love you ... it never ends.

VACKRA SVENSKA FLICKOR

Observing you, two beautiful
    Swedish girls called Ingrid and a
    friend at the Deutches Museum,
we engaged in human physics,
two college friends denying the
    existence of god
and senseless domestic inhibitions on a mission abroad.

We studied history, science, art and Svenska tullar,
and vackra Svenskar flickor won.

We later bought and unabashedly named an old Volksbug, 'Ingrid',
fondled her brazenly, drove our passions reckless
through luscious Europa's unquenchable body by day,
slept with the Ingrid who carried us and dreamed of embracing you.

SUE

Made explicit still, her wide brimmed hat and lovely dress
one pastel afternoon in May, came calling unexpected as I chose my
    journey forward on another path, our future
captured in a mutual, unexpected wave goodbye,
never never understood, never sans regret.

GINNA

Ginna spinning delight somewhere between cotton and blonde; gentle,
sweet, complicit in a prom or two,
we shared an assassination, a post-grad fraternity or two,
a sister's indiscretion, respected in cautions we observed.
Love, then hurt turned ruin to our possibilities
by choices innocent but uncommunicated either way,
cartography finite, personal, ours to explore for life.

JUNE

Summer fare and crested day is only made by wintering spring Growing
red till slow magic, supple leaves and heat begin;
The pictures drawn in May, conceived in March, sprouted in A-pril
Bring gawky birds alive, dancers in the woods, streams and party life
pour through abstraction to reality we know and share.
A life creating family, art and home from painted canvas, skin and

TESS

Tess is a female, fiercely alone,
spawning allure and irresistible desire,
a juggler of men, fueling their fire.
Tossing gifts toward their ends,
tossing flowers and fancy,
tossing caresses and perfume,
tossing their way to her, they aspire to presume
their dreams of her wanting for them were hers.
Men too often and their women, too,
realize her power and deceit too late;
Tess tossed her own.

EGG NOG

It's a selfish act of pleasure for me to break eggs, blend in spices, cream and spirits, watching for or having watched the passing of the Solstice, the full moon and the coming of the end of year.

From my youth to the reality of my experience, right here, right now; memories of dance and happiness, of sadness, longing, concern, defeat, epiphany and the sheer ecstasy of sharing and celebration -- with a fresh batch of Egg Nog.

So in this Season, let us decant the metaphors of renewal, reflection and sharing into thoughts of those we love and wishes for the best of health, joy, renewal, peace and plenty to all who share the wonder of life with us for the coming New Year.

As I remember it, my grandfather made this egg nog for holidays on the family farm in Indiana. My recipe is the closest thing to the taste I can summon up. Every time I make it, I remember something else, and add a shade of this or remove a tad of that, but the key ingredient in good egg nog is its spirit. No good egg nog was made just by following a recipe. The right taste requires thoughtfulness, attention to detail, clean tools and a bit of Zen luck. To begin, I head back to memories of the farm to get a good taste of the original. "You come too."

The house was built on a hill named Mt. Eschol by the "original" settlers, my family. The lane goes up the west slope past the old barns, sawmill and workshops toward the house. From the house down to the barn lot, there is a path where Grandpa shared the magic that a sled works fine on frosty grass even without snow early on a cold morning. It leads on up by the house past a well-used iron lunch bell hanging on posts.

We enter into one end of the screened-in back porch on the south side of the house. There's the wood-framed couch, where Grandpa napped after lunch in the summer before heading back to afternoon chores, and the rockers to sit and visit or to read the paper and the mail. The egg nog crock sits on the end of a long, cold stone step up to the kitchen door.

The kitchen door has a plain glass window. Set beside it are three floor-to-ceiling sashed glass windows making the whole south wall of the kitchen facing the back porch. Inside, the deep, green ceramic-over-iron sink is mounted on a thick walnut plank set against the pillars between the windows next to the stove. There's a dog bowl on the floor under it. Standing at the sink my Grandmother had a view out to the south, past the well house, through the locust trees in the yard, each with an old grade school desk bench beneath it. The view continues down the hill, across the corn field, to the meadow, creek and woods beyond.

Visible in the winter, across the creek through the gray woods' limbs, sits the long-abandoned, one-room school house Grandma attended, its massive foundation timbers laid on rock. Bats in the belfry, now, the blackboards below carry generations of chalked messages, lessons or not.

The creek runs southwest to northeast, all the way across the farm, mostly within the woods. Down the hill from the house as we look out the kitchen windows, the creek forms a boundary between the fields and woods, running through bluegrass, mayapple, thistle, berries and trees along both banks. In the summer, livestock forage loose in the woods. Groundhogs live in among the trunks of the sycamore and ash trees along the creek, with access to hickory, chestnut, oak, walnut, wild fruit, and roots - near enough to the cornfields but discreetly far enough away so as not to draw attention.

During the holidays, as I remember it, there is snow and a hard freeze on, so the ice pond down the hill to the east of the house is frozen. Depending on the time of day, the skaters may be pushing fresh snow off the ice, grooming it with an iron push-blade, or sitting in the shelter of an old, rough-sawn hog coop fronted with a fire. A four-foot thick willow tree has fallen away from the pond across the bank in such a way that it provides seating, plenty of hang space and marshmallow sticks.

Let's go on in and join the festivities. It may take a while to get through the kitchen, depending on who has arrived and the state of the hors d'oeuvres, the turkey, oyster dressing, pecan pie, &c. We go on through the kitchen, down the hall past the Symphonium, and put our coats in the bedroom at the end of the hall to the right. Take a peek out the North Door, brass crank-bell in the middle, across the fallow garden, the apple and persimmon trees, down the hill to the barns to the cattle in the feedlot and across the large pasture to the north.

Now we're on the last leg, heading past the stairs with the greatest sliding banister in the western world through the door to the dining room where the china five-generation wedding punchbowl stands on a corner table with a lace tablecloth. The crystal cups are all set out around it, and if you're lucky, Uncle Kenny has ladled out a cup for you already, hands the nutmeg over for a sprinkle, says your name, and there is the taste.

INGREDIENTS

A half dozen large, fresh eggs (brown ones feel better)
A half cup sugar (or stevia)
One & a half quarts heavy cream
3/4 cup golden rum (or lime in mango/apple cider)
A half cup peach brandy (or clementine in peach juice)
2 ounces Jack Daniels (or maple syrup)
1.5 ounces tequila (or clementine juice & pepper)
A half teaspoon instant expresso(!)
A quarter teaspoon salt (just !)
A half teaspoon vanilla (maybe a few drops more)
A quarter teaspoon fresh nutmeg & slightly less cinnamon
Tools: 2 ½ quart, wide-mouthed plastic pouring container with lid & spout; graduated pint cup; measuring spoons, egg beater.

- Wash the eggs; separate the yolks into the container and save the whites covered at room temperature. Contamination of the whites is a mortal sin. Six egg whites make about half a cup.
- Pour the sugar, rum, brandy, tequila, expresso, salt, vanilla, nutmeg and cinnamon into the container.
- Put on the lid, hold the spout and s h a k e (or beat) the mixture violently, turning the container so that the mixture inside "fluffs up" – use your judgment, but the more air you get in and the smoother the mix is, the better.
- Let it sit for about an hour in the coolest part of the room. Microscopic things are happening during this hour. The eggs are melding into the sugar and alcohol or citrus and the rawness is getting cooked out.
- After about an hour, pour in the whipping cream. Shake violently as before. Evenly space those molecules.
- The mixture forms a lattice so that the fat in the cream, the egg solids and the sugar are just rinsed by the liquor. Set the container aside.
- Whip the egg whites till they hold an egg-white wave: "stiff, but not dry." Open the container and pour in the egg whites on top of the mixture. Let the egg whites sit on the mixture in the container. DO NOT SHAKE. Put the container in the cold till you're ready to serve.

- When the time comes, shake the mixture violently again till the mixture's well dispersed, fluffy, and together but not homogenized.

Serve in 4-6 ounce cups with nutmeg. Shake before each pour.

www.ingramcontent.com/pod-product-compliance
Lightning Source LLC
Chambersburg PA
CBHW051238120626
46547CB00014B/1700